# Mood Swings

## Courtney Prudhomme

© 2015 Courtney Prudhomme
All rights reserved.

ISBN: **13:978-0692535295**
ISBN 10: **0692535292**
LCCN Imprint Name: Courtney Prudhomme
**Houston, Texas**

To everyone who has supported me—thank you! Special thanks to my mom, brother, family, and close friends. To Amber Simpson, Erik Moore, and Chelsea Jackson—thank you for helping me bring this book to life.

**Poem Titles**

1. Inconsistent
2. Life
3. Blue
4. Lies
5. All Things Go
6. Too Many Thoughts
7. Like a Clock
8. Changes
9. Love Affair
10. Damages
11. Higher Perspective
12. Unpredictable
13. Beautifully
14. First Dates
15. Opposites Attract
16. I'll Change
17. Risk
18. Been Crazy
19. Love
20. Blinded by Love
21. I Just Keep Asking
22. Overthinking
23. I'll Be Fine
24. Puzzles
25. The Real Me
26. Like Reality
27. In the City
28. Losing Touch
29. On My Brain
30. Things Change
31. Overdose
32. Lemons
33. Feelings

34. Missed Calls
35. Over
36. A Warm Summer
37. Chills
38. Mine Now
39. Experiences Turn to Memories
40. Same Story
41. Foggy
42. Last Night
43. Choices
44. Fly
45. Thoughts from a Balcony
46. Better than Getting Laid
47. Thoughts Are Rolling
48. Not Staying
49. Wordplay
50. Ceilings
51. Circles
52. Eyes and Lies
53. Ride with Me

I'm always wondering why life is bugging like a fly!

# Inconsistent

I'm up then I'm down
I leave then come back around
I'm fine then I'm tumbling to the ground
Internally screaming so there's no sound
I'm down then I'm up
Come back around like I'm stuck
Externally reaching until I'm struck
By everything us, I trust
Everything we created in lust

# Life

Then I look at myself like I'm somebody else
But I know I'm nobody else but myself
And when I'm down, I have to help myself
Because I know I can't depend on nobody else
If you want to read me
Take my heart off the shelf
Open me up until you see my emotions felt
If I'm too cold for you, I'll allow myself to melt
With your help
Put my arms around your body like a belt
We're just products of our environments
And we just play with the cards we're dealt

# Blue

Self-expression of my emotions
I'm just trying to live with the motion
Because the things I see got me seasick
There's too many waves in life's ocean
Life ashes rub off like lotion
That love shit never smelled like roses
Now I'm older; now I know this
And my silence was never golden
Maybe next time I should speak up
And then slide through like a Visa
The first time we intersected
Was the first time I got to meet you
So many things that life can teach you
The sky's the limit; I hope to reach you
All these feelings I let seep through
The wall in my heart; I'm feeling sea, blue

# Lies

You kept lying
And I keep trying
Not to lie in a bed full of lies
Leaving scars on my heart
Like they're embedded lies
I want us to grow
But we keep on dying
It hurts so much that it hurts
It hurts so much that we're crying
It hurts so bad that it's worse
It hurts so bad that we're dying
And you keep on lying
And I keep on trying
But I can't be a fool for you
I can't be a fool for a liar

# All Things Go

Cherish these days; man, do they go quick
Cherish these nights, 'cause that's when the time slips
Fall asleep and wake up, reminded of the same shit
I don't think they understand that this can be some fatal shit
I keep writing raps, it's like I'm making hits
On paper, but maybe later, I can record this shit
All things go; I need to reinvent
If you used to matter, I don't know what it really meant
I mean really, what did it really mean?
I guess all things go when it's not heaven-sent

# Too Many Thoughts

Too many thoughts; I'll be back in a few
My life is a trip; I got some packing to do
If life is a gift; I got some wrapping to do
Reality hits me; it had some slapping to do
Show a little gratitude; I still got magnitude
My mind is a mountain
And my thoughts reaching altitudes
Even though I walk around this bitch
With an attitude
Don't take it personal, baby
I'm not mad at you

It's like emotion on my sleeve, and it's been worn
I wear it like a fashion; now my shirt's torn
Because I wake up every day to a new storm
No alarm—just comes; it doesn't even warn
But I'm still the fucking best; I toot my own horn
But if you ever need a shoulder, I got two arms

# Like a Clock

On my mind like a thought
Going in circles like a clock
Times get hard like a rock
Comes at once like a flock
Makes my heart skip a beat
It's like my heart learned to hop
I'm under the influence
And I don't care to be on top
So I go like a clock; I don't stop, like a clock

# Changes

Changes in me that I hope that I'm around for
I can't push it to the side like I got time for it
I'm ahead of my time; it's like I time forward
Married to this life—legal rights; I didn't sign for it
Soon as the night hits, I lie more; I cry more
I give up every night, but every day I try more
Life is on my mind more; how will I strive for it?
A pretty face is just a face; I know I got to grind more
Time is growing up on me—probably why I sound sore
I'm at war; life is on the floor
I guess I have to thrive more
Jump in it—like dive more
But when I see the shit
I just get blind more
I can't believe the shit; it's like I die more
Life is a slow death; it's like I'm dying more
I'm too deep, so I drown more

# Love Affair

I lust, and I must—I just—I feel like I rushed
It was too much
And now I'm just blabbering and such
I have you on my mind, all the time; I can't sleep
I'm one with the one; I cannot flee
Touching me zealously
But rebelliously
Cupid shooting aimlessly right at my feet
Is love supposed to be?
What I envision in my sleep?
Because it seems that when I dream
It's of you lying next to me

# Damages

I know that damages have the ability to create more damage
But I thought that what was over was over
What was destroyed was destroyed
Having to learn from my emotions
That damages still drive like the motion
That I'm still blue as an ocean
That I'm still blue like the emotion
I feel so deeply that I'm soaking
In feelings the minute that I'm awoken

# Higher Perspective

You were sitting on my mind
While I was sitting on the clouds
Making love to my mind
Seeing things from my perspective
I'm on the wall like the time
I reflect on life but never mirror it
I learn through my experiences
And I don't want no interferences
Poetry is my resiliency
Pain lights up like a blunt
Feel so cold that you feeling it
My life feels like a stunt
Broken heart—I'm on the run
Shit is tough; I'm almost done
This weighs a ton
I'm feeling numb
Being triggered like a gun

# Unpredictable

I know life's about making it through
When I look back at my life
I'm aware that I grew
I see life changes, and I swear that I'm new
I know life's about faking it too
I know life is short, and I'm facing that too
I make a promise to myself
And I'm breaking that too
I can't trust myself; I'm unpredictable too

# Beautifully

Stay friends with her, and I risk falling deeper
And since I don't have her, I can't keep her
Should I delete her? From this memory of mine
'Cause I swear she's on my mind
When she shouldn't be
It must be the crazy things she do to me
My heart beats, but this time, not ruthlessly
I'm falling, damn it—I'm falling beautifully

# First Dates

First dates are like a test; did I pass or not?
I couldn't tell if the time was beating fast or not
It's like you had me on the moon
Like an astronaut
While my heart was beating fast in knots

We intersected when we were introduced
Back in March, when we were introduced
You came in smiling; I was smiling too
You said I looked you up and down
And that was probably true
I mean
Just look at you

## Opposites Attract

Opposites attract in so many ways
Go with the flow like ocean waves
You found my heart in many pieces
Look at the many pieces you've saved
I know that things can change
In a couple of days
I had to stop giving brain
To the one on my brain
Or things would never change
Until things start making sense to me
Now it's all making sense to me

# I'll Change

Look at what you did to me
You're so into me, so good to me
You're a lover and a friend to me
Just look at what you did to me
Thoughts from a balcony
Thinking to myself
I was once so lost
Thought I'd never come back to me
I found me; then I found you—right after me
And I hope nobody comes after me
I hope that I get a chance to be a better me
I was the blue sea, but things can get better, see
I said, I love you—I love you, and I'll let you be
But I can't set us free
Not ready—not yet
I'll change—I'll change, you'll see
I'll change like moods
I'll change like minds
I'll change like a switch
I'll change like time
I'll change like cents
I'll change like signs
I'll change like things
Like the leaves, I'll fall
Into spring
You'll see
I'll change

# Risk

I know it sounds bad, but it feels way worse
Spent my whole life running from love
Until I met her
Spent some time running until I met her worth
And her worth was worth the risk of getting hurt
And that's probably what hurts the worst
'Cause I was willing to give it up
Put some trust in us
This one was for love
'Cause every time I thought of her
It made me blush
Every time I felt her fingers brush
It gave me such a rush
So when she ended things between us
I couldn't help but feel crushed
That we lost to love
And made love to lust

# Been Crazy

I know your days been crazy, and nights been harder
And this is bigger than life; this is clearer than water
She shines on me like light
I tripped the first time I saw her
Then I eventually fell
The script was flipped like quarters
She was digging into me deep, and I think
How am I supposed to sleep?
How will I make it?
When every part of me is getting steeper
When I know she's falling deeper
Then I look at her; she smiles
Then the moment becomes sweeter
I don't care what my mind thinks
My heart allows me to be freer
But my mind, this mind of mine
Keeps me in a sinker
My heart's changing lanes
But I can't even find the blinkers
Hear my heartbeat; it's the bass in life's speakers

# Love

Our love sunk to the bottom of the ocean
I tried to save it; I dived in, but I kept floating
I couldn't reach it; we couldn't keep it
Now I can't even sleep
So I can't even dream
I'm stuck here
Looking at the flow of the ocean
I'm going through the motions
With different emotions
'Cause I left my heart open
I'm hoping
I'm wishing
Everything will be golden
I'm a fool for your love
And I'm sure it makes no sense
I know that you love me—I know this; I know this
So let's start from scratch and regrow this
Let's focus

# Blinded by Love

It took a weekend for me to realize it was real in our eyes
It took one kiss for me to realize all this time I was blind
It took one gust—just one's trust—to make me fall for us
It took one rush—just one touch—to make some room for us
It took one hug—just one drug—to make some room for love
Take up all the space in my mind 'cause you're all I'm thinking of
You're all I'm thinking of, and I hope you feel the same
I'm so afraid of getting hurt 'cause I know that things can change
But one thing I know for sure: that my feelings will remain
But a second thing for sure: in my life, I'm glad you came
I knew we had a shot, but love has never been a game
You were a spark of interest, but I was waiting on the flame
It took a weekend for me to realize it was real in our eyes
It took one kiss for me to realize all this time I was blind
Just one gust—just one's trust—to make me fall for us
Just one rush—just one touch—to make me fall for love

# I Just Keep Asking

Is it real? Tell me what it is—is it real?
Tell me how you feel if it's real
You're head over heels
Time will reveal
You're running through my mind
And my mind is a field
Wasted like a spill
My mind is a track
Thoughts piling like a stack
'Cause love is a trip like vacation
Puts you on a trip; you got to pack
Puts you on the map
Cupid throwing arrows at my back

# Overthinking

I'm overthinking; I'm overthinking
I'm analyzing my way of thinking
The things I'm seeing—I can barely blink
Always a pen in my hand, body full of ink
I had a long week, but I don't need a drink
'Cause I'm higher than a peak
And I'm off my feet
Been up all week, and I need some sleep
'Cause I'm full of dreams, and I overthink

# I'll Be Fine

I'll be fine sipping wine alone when shit is on my mind
It just gives me the opportunity to paint what's on my mind
Or maybe what's in it
My mind then shifted
My high gives me higher thoughts
My mind is lifted
Understand why I'm so down!
Don't try to lift me
I'm misunderstood; nobody gets me
I'm a catch, but they always miss me
My life's a sketch, but the picture's written
My wordplay nasty, the way my thoughts are spitting
It's the creation and creativity of my nature—
please forgive me

# Puzzles

Arranging me like pieces
Losing pieces
I'm puzzled
My mind is a cell 'cause my thoughts are that troubled
Try to get it together, put my life in a huddle
Spoon my girl like utensils, ease my mind in the cuddle
Throw my thoughts in the puddle
Throw my pain in the struggle
No time to be subtle
Work it out like a muscle
I got a fistful of knuckles
Fuck it all—fuck 'em; fuck 'em!!

# The Real Me

She says, "I want to know the real you"
But I'm stuck in the past like rearview
Introspecting, reflecting like a mirror
When you find something real
That's when it hits you
Like a bullet that's coming from a pistol
Feeling high…now I'm launching like a missile
I'm allergic to life…no tissue nearby
I'm so fucking blessed, I need some tissue
My words speak volumes, but I got issues
Life blows like whistles, and I miss you
What is life? Shit got me so mental
Higher than a kite; it's all in my mental

# Like Reality

Like reality, it slaps me
That you don't want to see me happy
So my attitude is snappy
Fuck the world, I am nappy
When life hits me, it impacts me
My pain is crack, and I'm an addict
I lose my balance; I'm a habit
Hop on beats like I'm a rabbit
Wrecking beats until it's tragic
Wrecking beats until I'm crashing
I'm distracted, stuck in traffic
Life's a joke; sometimes I'm laughing
Wear me out like I'm a fashion
Fuck me wild with so much passion
Fuck my words and make them actions
Fire burns; I flick the ashes

# In the City

Let's go take a walk in the city
Surrounded by all these buildings
The wind blows, and it's chilly
Holding hands, surrounded by feelings
Love works in mysterious ways
Bringing two souls together
The ways
It came, I was so oblivious
From curious to serious days
The universe is a mysterious place
We never let our experiences fade
These are experiences that we made
Intimate nights became memories made
Deep into the night, everything becomes vivid
Coming for my heart; knock knock—who is it?
It's usually when the past tries to visit
But we made it, baby, we did it
Where the wind blows, and it's chilly
Where we're surrounded by all these buildings
Where the streetlights are plenty
Where we can find the secrets to life
Because I'm pretty—sure, there's many
Let's take a walk in the city

# Losing Touch

Start thinking that I'm losing touch
I need to get a grip, and I'm in a rush
Losing her—every hour, every touch
Damn, getting better is a must
My heart feeling like it's crushed
Life is rough
Can make relationships tough
My heart is full of fear right now
It's like our love's corrupt
Fuck
Let me put in all my trust
I trust that we can make it through
I trust that we can make it through
Even when we feel blue, we can make it through
'Cause I got these feelings for you
And I can't filter them through
'Cause like leaves, we blew; like seeds, we grew
Into something new

# On My Brain

Yea, all this stress on my brain, right
My heart is walking with legs right
No romance—just candlelight
I spilled the Sprite; I take a million flights
I need time to think like a million nights
This nipsey hustle got me feeling right
I lose sight until time kills
Time moves forward so time killed
I'm bipolar with no pills
I have stress on my brain like no chill
I'm numb to it all, like no feel
Living life with no shield
I'm so gone, but I'm so here
It's like I've been high for a whole year
Yea, all this stress on my brain here
All this stress on my brain here

# Things Change

Things change like the seasons
Cupid came aiming while I was sleeping
I woke up to emotions on my sleeve
The wall in my heart broke in pieces
I woke up to the girl of my dreams
Took my breath away; I couldn't breathe
Swept me off my feet; I couldn't leave
Thinking to myself, This is a dream

# Overdose

I was addicted; I do admit it
Nothing was the same
I just wished things would've changed
But they didn't
Nothing could compare to the life that we're living
My love becomes a drug
And my mind then went missing
I get high in these clouds and just listen
Sick and tired of being in mental prisons
Without you by my side
It's like the sun is hidden
So I let my mind drift off into the night
Reaching new heights
I'm overdosing on you

# Lemons

The lemons in my life make the worst lemonade
Maybe I need sugar to make it sweet
To help the bitterness fade
My visions fade as I watch as these feelings fade
Picasso of the mind
I draw conclusions when I illustrate
My words are artistry; every time I write
My pencil paints
I'm numb; then my feelings paint
I'm numb; then my feelings faint

# Feelings

Feelings come and go
Or maybe they're suppressed
I don't know that I suppress
Even though I do it best
I hate the feeling of uneasiness
The feeling of unrest
I need a bulletproof vest
'Cause her heart is in my chest
And these feelings feel like death
Staring at the ceiling when these feelings make me sweat
Now I'm staring at the mirror; she left her feelings on my neck
It all seemed appealing; I trusted feelings when we met—"Hey, how you're doing, glad to have you as my guest"
The more time we spent
The more the feelings progressed
The more the feelings erected
You deserved my heart, not anything less
'Cause all I needed to survive was your love in my chest
I would have protected it all with my bulletproof vest
'Cause the harder I fall, the more I invest
When the nighttime falls, I tend to express
I could've had it all, but then I left

# Missed Calls

Missed calls and e-mails
All going into details
Selling me deliberated lies like retail
You sell me the same lies
The same lies that she sells
The same lies that he tells
We're going into details
We will have to see hell in order to see hell
The only thing between us is a seashell
I'm falling like the leaves, well
We hear the police, jail
I hope he doesn't notice the smell
Wait, it's a female

# Over

Look at you with bitter eyes
I'm tired of trying to make this work
Moving on like ocean tides
You couldn't see what I was worth
All you did was make things worse
Looked at me with troubled eyes
Treated me like I was dirt
I'm about to get what I deserve
You failed to see what I was worth
I'm moving on; I'm leaving first
This love is dead; my feelings surf
I got to put my feelings first
Look at you with bitter eyes
I've tried and tried to make this work
I've died trying to make this work
I've died trying to make this work

# A Warm Summer

A warm summer in a cold world
Blow smoke as my pen twirls
Fast forward, like I'm a movie
I will act an ass
Like I'm a booty
Reveal the naked truth
Like I'm a nudist
I think the air outside just made my mood shift
Wind blowing, just made my mood drift
A new episode; it's like I flew here
I'm new here; I'm finally landing
I feel indifferent
And I cannot stand it
Mind control
And I cannot panic
These words are frantic
My mind is slanted
Thoughts jumping in my head like they're dancing
Thoughts jumping in my head throwing tantrums
Thoughts jumping in my head like ranting
Thoughts jumping in my head like panting

# Chills

When I first saw you
I was thinking maybe we can chill
To see if we could fall into something real
The attraction was beyond surreal
Our looks revealed
Lips closed; now lips revealed
Now you're touching me in ways
Giving me the chills
Fucking me for days
Giving me the feels

# Mine Now

Emotions felt
My heart is more alive now
I want to make love to you
Kiss it slowly; take my time now
Say my name one more time
Now help me lose my mind now
Falling into a trance
It's beautiful how you're mine now

# Experiences Turn to Memories

Experiences turn to memories that eventually get boring
Morning clouds are roaring
Then it eventually starts pouring
Psychological soaring
In a world that becomes so foreign
I'm awakened by these feelings
When the rest of the world is snoring
Turning stories and experiences into poetry
They say the mind is a beautiful thing
When I look in the mirror
I know mine is gorgeous
I clear my mind of all distortions
I'm feeling all the forces
Why you on my case like the courts?
Shit gets messy like divorces
She runs my mind like courses
She rides my mind like horses
I visualize the distorted—ceiling high, I'm out of orbit

# Same Story

It's the same story, same words on the page
Where is my sane? Am I in it?
Insane
It's my story, my life, my rain
You can see my rain on the windowpane
It blends so well that you can hardly tell
Everything in me camouflage with the rain
Bottled these emotions so they're saved
Texts from my cell got me feeling like hell
Like everything in me just blew up in flames

# Foggy

Thoughts are foggy
I don't think they're clear yet
Dirty mind; clear my mind like Windex
The words come to me naturally like reflex
Pure creativity with no syntax
Fuck them rules; I always bend that
Where the trees at?
Blowing strong
High as fuck
Where the breeze at?
I keep it cool, like relax
Laid back until I relapse
Last night she had me on my kneecaps
I made her feel something new, no recaps

# Last Night

Last night we made a movie
Views from a TV
My mind swings like a monkey
A new branch
Sometimes a new tree
If you don't know me now
You never knew me
'Cause I'm the shit like dookie
My words come out so smoothly
I use these words so loosely
We chill like smoothies
Outside the box—don't lose me
I know I get confusing
I'll be the sun, then blue sea
My wordplay is purely juicy
Thoughts in my head like "choose me"
Like "write my thought down!"
My emotions try to move me

# Choices

Tongue twisted from life's contradictions
Every day is a life-or-death decision
Please don't make no reckless decision
I can't see from your view
And I don't want your vision
I'm getting so far in life
I swear I'm in it
So deep, I swear I'm swimming
So deep
I lost some perspective
Life choices
Time to make a selection
Like an election
So many choices—I'm stressing
Somewhere stuck between blessings
I'm rich in thoughts I'm investing
Strip my thoughts of insanity until I'm undressing
My soul so restless
Thoughts hang like a necklace

# Fly

Sometimes I wish that I could fly
Sometimes I get high as the sky
Heart on my chest just like a tie
It's 3:14, just like a pi
Heart is in pieces like a pie
It's so much water in my mind
I'm always flowing; I'm never dry
My thoughts are pouring from my eyes
Up and down like a ride
Go buy some papers; roll like tide
Unaware like hypnotize
Hypothesize what's on my mind
Every day I leave my mark before I die
I'm on the rise

# Thoughts from a Balcony

The woman right next to me
I know that she's aware of me
Thoughts from a balcony
Luckily, you welcome me
You know I'm crazy for my fuzzy honey
Like a bumblebee
You humble me, pick me back up
And then you fumble me
You leave me there alone, cold
Then you come run to me
This became a game
Honestly, this is no fun to me
I knew this would happen
I knew I'd be no exception
You've had me caught up in your web of deception
Since its inception

Everything is real—what I feel, I believe in
I didn't see this coming, but I wish I would have seen it
Even if I would've seen it, I probably wouldn't have believed it
Below the rose, a concrete grows
A beautiful tragedy
When a beautiful woman
Comes welcome me from a balcony
It baffles me
The way she stares at me
Is this fair to me?
She looks like the truth
I'm there stuck in a fallacy

# Better than Getting Laid

We made love for the first time yesterday
It was better than getting laid
I'm not worried about getting played
'Cause your love feels like when I wake up
And I just got paid
First fire, first flame
Been burning for you since the first date
Had me feeling like I was in fourth grade
So many thoughts about you
And I'm only on the first page

# Thoughts Are Rolling

Thoughts are rolling like I'm bowling
Go through a maze just like a rodent
My thoughts are poets
And my mind knows this
No one notice
But now I notice
I'm in my moment
And as a poet
I try to own this
My thoughts are potent
I don't write on paper
I only fold it
I don't write on paper
I only roll it
My thoughts are loaded
I feel like boo-boo
But smell like roses

# Not Staying

I'm not staying in this misery
I'm tired of guessing
I'm tired of being stuck in your mystery
I'm tired of stressing
Time changes blessings
Time to accept it
Acceptance
'Cause I'm tired of my heart and mind wrestling
'Cause you're interjecting
With my flow
And I know it's time for me to go
I came to this decision slow
The moment's cold; my heart is snow
We still had seeds that needed to grow
Being happy with you that was seasons ago
A year ago
Some tears ago
Now I'm letting go

# Wordplay

My feelings in the background
Way beyond adolescence
But this paper is my playground
And my wordplay is so fucking childish
I'm an animal first; I'm wild
Eyes wide open like an owl
The truth hits me like a foul
That love sucks, and I want to bash it
But I still love you, so I still have it
I got to move on 'cause time passes
But it's happening slow, so time's dragging
Time's lagging
I need to get away on a trip with no baggage

# Ceilings

The ceilings cry
I'm on the clouds
I'm ceiling high
I'm on the stars
I'm sitting high
Never down
Live in the sky
Like I can fly
The more I try
I try to move
To dust it off
Like I'm a broom
Then I start swinging
Like I'm a mood
Now I need some space
Like I'm out of room
Or I'll act an ass
Like I'm a moon

# Circles

I must be out of my mind
The way she got me going in circles
Or maybe I'm losing my mind
The way she got me jumping over hurdles
I mean, this girl is on my mind
All of my thoughts of her become verbal
So close to the finish line
But the finish line is in circles
And as soon as I hear your voice
I fall under
And I wonder
What nature feels like without the thunder?
Then I fall into a slumber
My heart is beating—drummer
Racing like a runner
I wonder
If my heart is getting dumber
I wonder
Sometimes when I'm alone, I just ponder
We're in this ocean in a circular motion
Time to take me under
I must be out of my mind
The way she got me going in circles
Or maybe I'm losing my mind
The way I'm jumping over these hurdles

# Eyes and Lies

All lies on the bed
All lies in my head
The truth lies in my head
All lies that I dread
All eyes on us
All eyes on lust
All lies on love
All lies on lust
My eyes on love
My eyes on us
Fuck in the back
Like we're riding on the bus
Passing up stops
We're not in a rush
Stimulate my mental
So many thoughts to discuss

# Ride with Me

Ride with me, or get high with me
I'm slow to trust; take your time with me
I try to understand in life the finer things
But I wake up every morning being reminded of things
And now I'm forced to deal with all these timely things
While trying to block out what's inside of me
It seems like everything inside of me
Is dying in me
It's either you ride or get high with me
Get higher than the sky with me
I'm feeling—I roll up, I roll up, I'm chilling
Go sit in my car, and get on top of the hill
I'm healing
I go up and get high as the ceiling
As soon as I do
I get the fuck out my feelings

Your brain is the most powerful and most important sex organ you've got, so get that mind right!

www.ingramcontent.com/pod-product-compliance
Lightning Source LLC
Chambersburg PA
CBHW021000090426
42736CB00010B/1397